CONTENTS

GROW UP!

Every day
in every way
I grow
a little more

Older, higher,
wider too,
and further
from the floor

My head,
my hands,
my knees,
my nose,
my teeth,
my tongue,
my toes

So steadily
so silently
my body
slowly

GRRRRRRROWS!

A HANDFUL

One *finger*
two *finger*
three *finger*
four

all little friends
but wait
there's more –

one stubby chum
hey, that's your *thumb*

Now off they go
for a *handful* of *fun*...

*THUMBS UP!
HIGH FIVE!
REACH WAY UP TO THE SKY!*

Four little *fingers*
add one *thumb* –

and what
have you got...?

A *handful*
of *FUN!*

A TICKET TO KALAMAZOO!

We bought
  a ticket
    to *KALAMAZOO*

*We went by train
  by boat, by plane
    around the world
     and back again*

*Through night and day
  through sun and rain
    through mist and snow*

  Then where did we go?

We bought
  a ticket
    to *TIMBUKTU*

We went by train
   by boat, by plane
      around the world
        and back again

Through night and day
   through sun and rain
      through mist and snow

    Then where did we go?

We bought
   a ticket
      to *KATMANDU*

    We went by train,
      by boat, by plane... (chorus)

    Then where did we go?

     HOME
     SWEET
     HOME!

Elephant Beat

Fancy a ride on an ELEPHANT?

Bobbing to the rhythm
of the elephant beat
as it pounds round town
on those four great feet

With its great grey ears
and its great grey trunk
what a blast as you pass
on that great grey hunk

Fancy a ride on an ELEPHANT?

Better than a tiger
better than a whale
better than a ride
on a mighty snail

Better than a train
or a plane or a bike
when you're bob-bob-bobbing
anywhere you like!

Fancy a ride on an ELEPHANT?

Those ears may flap
that trunk may honk
that tail may swish
on that great grey hunk

Now do watch out
for it may have a wash
so you might get splashed
with a splishity-splosh!

Fancy a ride on an ELEPHANT?

What a hoot it'll be, all tickety-boo
when you're on board, so come on, you!

*FANCY A RIDE
ON AN ELEPHANT?*

The Terrible Ten

1 do a stroll like a **tiger**

2 do a grrr like a **bear**

3 do a scuttle like a **spider**

4 do a leap like a **hare**

5 do a stretch like a **lion**

6 do a flap like a **bat**

7 do a swoop like a **barn owl**

8 do a nibble like a **rat**

9 do a sway like an **eagle**

10 do a cluck like a **hen**

Then it might be nice
just once or twice
to do the *ten*
AGAIN!

Fuss! Fuss! Fuss! or The GOLDILOCKS Rap

Everybody, everywhere –
please listen to me
and hear my tale of the 3 Bears 3
and the fussiest girl you ever did see
who went by the name of Little Miss G.

Now G went out for a walk one day
when after a while she lost her way
and deeper and deeper into the wood
she followed the smell of something good.

She found inside a dreamy cottage
three hot bowls of creamy porridge. Fuss! Fuss! Fuss!
One too lumpy. One too hot.
But one just right. She scoffed the lot. Fuss! Fuss! Fuss!

The first two chairs? She wasn't sure.
The third just tumbled to the floor. Fuss! Fuss! Fuss!
So next those beds. In number 3
young G would nap so peacefully. Fuss! Fuss! Fuss!

The bears came back before too long,
crying, 'WHAT THE DING DONG'S GOING ON!?'
On finding G in Baby's bed
it made those 3 Bears 3 see red.

'Yo, Goldie – this ain't cool. It's rude.
You can't sleep here or steal our food!
We need our breakfast! Cook some more –
you lazybod, you know the score.'

Never in that dreamy cottage
had such bowls of yummy porridge
been prepared by anyone.
The bears cried, 'Goldie – oh what fun

to start a porridge take-away!'
And so they did. Without delay.
The queues were long. Went up the hill.
And far away. Then further still.

For ever after, our Miss G
cooked porridge with the 3 Bears 3
and happily – but fussily...

FUSS!

FUSS!

FUSS!

13

Scratch and Sniff Bear

The bear came down
  from the mountain
    yawning the morning away

And scratching
  and sniffing
and stretching
  and itching
and fishing
  for most of the day

The bear went
  into the forest
    hoping to find some tea

And stuffing
  and sticking
and picking
  and licking
the honey
  he took from a tree

14

The bear went back
   to the mountain
      yawning from having his fun

And hopping
   and skipping
and humming
   and singing
and happy
   with food in his tum
with honey and fish
   so *YUM!*

THE BUG HOTEL

Been busy buzzing all day long?
Or heaving balls of steaming dung?

Or have you lost your zip or sting?
Or need a break from everything?

It's time to leave your hill or hive.
To rest, relax, re-energise.

We'll pamper you. We'll treat you well.
We'll spoil you at *The Bug Hotel.*

We welcome all you beastly bugs –
from itchy nits to grotty grubs.

Our cleaners do their very best
to leave your room a total mess.

Do come and try our snuggly beds –
they're massive piles of rotting veg.

Hey, what's that icky, yucky smell?
We're proud to say *The Bug Hotel.*

Our kitchen stocks the freshest food
from local farms – organic poop.

A compost heap's our restaurant.
Our swimming pool's a swampy pond.

So laze away, come scoff, come dine.
Come shed your skin. De-stress. Unwind.

It's
filthy dirty,
stinks as well –
what not to love...?

THE BUG HOTEL

Busy Bugs

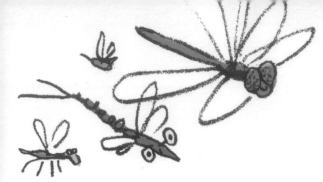

Out in the garden
look down low
see all the busy bugs
come and go. . .

tiny bugs
that feed on leaves

merry bugs
that buzz all day

shiny bugs
that creep up trees

scaredy bugs
that whizz away

fancy bugs
that chirp in grass

wiggly bugs
that hide in sand

bouncy bugs
that leap so fast

tickly bugs
that like your hand

Out in the garden
look down low
see all the busy bugs
come and go. . .

CONVERSATION WITH A FLY

ZZZZ!

Oh, hello, fly!

ZZZZ!

What are you up to, then?

ZZZZ!

Sorry, I didn't catch that...

ZZZZ!

No, I still didn't get it.

ZZZZ!

Are you trying to tell me something?

ZZZZ!

Something important, perhaps?

ZZZZ!

Is something the matter, maybe?

ZZZZ!

Are you in some kind of trouble?

ZZZZ!

Look. I don't understand 'ZZZZ!'

ZZZZ!

Please don't keep saying 'ZZZZ!'

ZZZZ!

Right, fly. I'll give you one more chance, okay?

zzzzzZZZZZZZZZZZ!!!

19

THREE LITTLE RIDDLES

Pond Poem

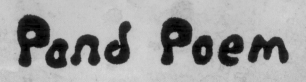

Once I was
a little dot.
Now I wriggle
such a lot.

Soon I'll have
a song and sing it.
Then you'll hear my
ribbit ribbit!

Can you guess?
I bet you can –
I'm a *TAD*....
yes I am!

I Wish

I've fingers five
though I've no hand –

no head, no brain.
D'you understand –

I cannot shine
though I'm a *star*?

I cannot swim
though I'm a *fish*?

Can I make sense?
Oh, how I wish!

Me, I am a
STA .....?

Little-by-Little Fish

Little by little
the little fish grew.
Little by little
as little fish do.

A flipper, a fin,
a flapper or two.
Skin all shimmery,
shiny and blue.

And moodier, yes,
and toothier too.
As many more gnashers
appeared anew.

Way down in the dark
that little fish grew
into a *SH...!*
As little fish do....

Ginger-Pincher

When moon is high
she heads on out
to hit the town
to snoop about

The world's asleep
so no one knows
can see her creep
on tippy-toes

Or marvel
at that rusty fur
or bushy
fuzzy tail of hers

So Ginger's off
to go a pinchin'
snout-a-sniffin'
whiskers twitchin'

She'll be sneakin'
round the shops
raidin' bins
for bits 'n bobs

She's so fearless
she's
RED FOX...!

Night Soup

(a simple recipe)

Take . . .

A slither of moon
a nip in the air
a sprinkle of stars
a creak from a stair

Add plenty of dark
the slink of a cat
(with cold green eyes)
a loop from a bat

The patter of rain
the whine of a dog
the taste of a dream
the wisp of a fog

24

The whoosh of a train
a sniff or a snore
the swoop of an owl
then stop – no more

Now let it go cold
and serve quite late
and all
that
is left
to do
is
W A I T...

SPACE POEM

The *sun* is like
a **gold** balloon

the *moon*
a **silver** pearl

the *earth* is like
a marble **blue**

the *milky way*
a **creamy** swirl

If *stars* are like
those little boats

afloat a *sea*
of night

the dark is when
a hand comes down

and switches
off **the light**!

One Little Alien

I'm
a little alien,
cute and green,
the grooviest
guy you've
n e v e r
seen -
! speedy like !
!! a meteor, sparky !!
!! like a star, spooky like !!
!! a moonbeam, gleaming !!
!! from afar. I whizz round !!
!! Jupiter, Saturn and !!
!! the sun. Yeah, !!
??? I'm a little ???
alien, life
is fun!

HUG DAY

Is today a long day?
A going-on-and-on day?
An everything's-all-wrong day?

You   need   a   hug.

Is today a worry day?
A knot-inside-your-tummy day?
A frowny, frumpy, grumpy day?

You   need   a   hug.

Is today a tough day?
A huff and a puff day?
A have-you-had-enough day?

Hey, you – me too –

let's have a

H U G !

28

HAPPY POEM

Happy as a rainbow
happy as a bee
happy as a dolphin
splashing in the sea

Happy as a holiday
down on the beach
happy as a sunflower
happy as a peach

Happy as a bunny
happy as a spoon
dripping with honey
happy as June

Happy as a banjo
plucking on a tune
happy as a Sunday
lazy afternoon

Happy as a memory
shared by two
happy as me. . .
when I'm with you!

29

For everyone everywhere who helps bring out the reader in every child.
And that includes uber-librarian by name and nature, Denise Reed.

'Hug Day' is for Karen and all the lovely Salters; remembering Ian
and welcoming Ren to the world.
JC

For Lena and Maja.

NL

Text copyright © James Carter 2023
Illustrations copyright © Neal Layton 2023
First published in Great Britain and the USA in 2023 by
Otter-Barry Books, Little Orchard, Burley Gate, Herefordshire, HR1 3QS
www.otterbarrybooks.com

A catalogue record for this book is available from the British Library
Designed by Arianna Osti

FSC
www.fsc.org
MIX
Paper from
responsible sources
FSC® C104723

ISBN 978-1-91307-410-4
Illustrated with pencil, ink and digital media

Set in Gotham
Printed in China

9 8 7 6 5 4 3 2 1